Muse-Sick

a music manifesto in
fifty-nine notes

Ian Brennan

Foreword by John Waters
Photos by Marilena Umuhoza Delli

Muse-Sick: a music manifesto in fifty-nine notes
Ian Brennan
© 2021
This edition © 2021 PM Press.

ISBN: 978–1–62963–909–3
Library of Congress Control Number: 2021936595

Cover by John Yates / www.stealworks.com
Interior design by briandesign
All photos © Marilena Umuhoza Delli

10 9 8 7 6 5 4 3 2 1

PM Press
PO Box 23912
Oakland, CA 94623
www.pmpress.org

Printed in the USA.

for Occhi di Luce

Along the Mussolini-widened street,
your mother hand-rolled pasta with love
while spitting words of hate.

The brevity of this book is not for want of material but is highly intentional. Anyone mistaking word count for worth is kindly directed to my previous two music books, which exceed seven hundred pages collectively.

Please note: This book is written during a time when venture capitalists are investing hundreds of millions of dollars each to gobble up aging superstars' song and record catalogues as if they were oil rights. These monetary over-lords have no intention for the music they now own to *ever* be naturally turned over and left fallow—as any sustainable ecosystem should or else face erosion and extinction.

Driven by economics rather than culture, these financial czars want nothing more than for our future to look much like our past.

Prologue

With enough time,
even faith becomes a dog name.

Somebody got to her, long ago
I could see it floating, untethered
deep in her eyes,
taunting strangers like a
"kick me" sign.

I still bear Sammy Hagar scars, misled musically from the start.

Like so many things, what we hoped would heal us only made us sicker. Singing along like whispering a prayer, we tried to make our soul match the songs.

My early life was lit by my mother's faltering searchlight heart. On a Christmas Day going home from the psychiatric ward, she stood, hesitating on our front porch. Unable to cross even that shallow threshold, she was obscured by more than the closed screen door.

This was all back when the city was still small. Before the skyline hid the skyline.

Though the bruise on her bicep was purple, it did not appear regal but dethroned. And for years it never seemed to fade. That history has only now begun to settle in me.

Decades later, turning cancer gray, our father's was an execution staid. We counted time in hours instead of days and, at sunrise, watched our phones.

Heading home at the train station, a baby boomer bore an oversized peace sign on her chest like a shield. It came as no surprise when she screamed "Fuck you!" in my face over a taxi turn.

My daughter's first word was not a word at all but a phrase.

"One-Note Foreword"

by John Waters

Here are ten reasons why this is a good book.

1) It's a radical protest, like Martin Luther's thesis nailed to the door of the Catholic church in 1517. Ready to rumble. Looking for a fight.
2) The author, Ian Brennan, is a purist. Almost to the point of sadism. His extreme opinions hurt but they hurt so well.
3) I can't sing, play an instrument, read sheet music, or even whistle, but I know good music when I hear it, and so does he.
4) Ian's wrong sometimes too, but that makes reading this manifesto more fun because you want to argue, challenge, punch him in his opinionated nose.
5) He hates money, which can be a problem in the business of show, yet he'll explain how to succeed without it.
6) He's against pop stars too, and isn't that refreshing?
7) His writing is depressing *and* funny. When you read in context that he's discovered that some Down syndrome singers "could act like assholes too," you won't be offended. You'll be enlightened.
8) He understands punk rock completely.

9) The author knows that "middle ground" is the most dangerous territory on earth. Biting the corporate hand is Ian's career advice, and he's made it work for himself, so why not you?

10) Mr. Brennan's a good psychiatrist, and the fifty-nine-minute music session that this book actually is will leave you feeling cured, musically adjusted, ready to open your ears to new music in a whole new way.

Introduction

99 Problems
(and Jay-Z is one)

There is an odd spiritual trade that transpires globally. Developing nations receive our physical castoffs while we siphon their culture as hand-me-ups. Through this twisted system, materialism spirals downward, while art ascends—first stolen, then claimed.

When a person alleges that someone is "the best living writer/artist/singer," what they really mean is the "one of the best *known* _____." To state otherwise is to exclude the scores of amazing individuals that go unnoticed or unheard.

Defenders of the meritocracy myth are like Darwinism enthusiasts (who ironically usually don't believe in evolution). Through victim blaming, they distance themselves from the brutality of systems of inequality.

Music critics today are so obsessed with appearing populist that they often deny their true tastes and become closet elitists, writing think pieces about the latest Disney-bred-and-fed pop star while secretly listening to Einstürzende Neubauten.

Building a culture around the underdog allows everyone to believe that *they* too are one regardless of their privilege. This pretense provokes suspicion about anything of depth culturally being elitist. The derision of whatever is deemed "liberal" recodes social progress as threatening and inspires the populace to police and censor each other, thus narrowing the field of possible inquiry further to suppress free speech as all cults do.

During my decades in the entertainment industry, I've encountered parades of faces hardened by too easy a life—individuals all knotted up inside, trying to be something they are not.

Equality is often mistaken as "treating everyone the same." Instead, it requires actively ensuring that every person is provided the same basic opportunities. If an individual who has less opportunity is treated the same as another who is privileged or already "made," the result is not equality but a perpetuation of a rigged game.

I do "see color." And, statistically speaking, it's quite likely that I tend to prefer people that aren't white, along with anyone that is marginalized.

Racism is a real-life horror story based on a fiction. Genetically, there is only one race: the human race.

We don't need more storytellers but more *truth*-tellers. Any culture steeped in fiction can't help but teeter toward delusion.

If upon seeing a camera for the first time, "primitive" tribes feared that having their photos taken would steal their soul, then Tom Cruise, Will Smith, and scores of other overexposed celebrities prove that hypothesis correct.

Through field recording, my goal is to create more space for the absent.

Instead, in the West, the T-shirt logo's life is longer than the band's.

The Source of All Sonic Sins

Before mirrors,
rivers and lakes.
Before vinyl and tape,
mountain canyon replays.

Often the generosity of approval that well-to-do foreigners lavish on "exotic" performers is as misguided as a visitor to America regarding a badly rendered version of the intro to "Stairway to Heaven" as a stunning artistic achievement and exclaiming, "We *totally* have to record that."

Idolatry is simply dehumanization's flipside.

Cross-cultural exchanges often sport patronizing praise and pedestal placement, the same distorted interpretations that lead to evaluating soccer players and super models as "intelligent" if they can speak in semicoherent sentences with a few multisyllabic words thrown in.

Whether traveling to more remote places like South Sudan or Transylvania or exploring voices closer to home like with the homeless community in my birthplace, Oakland, our goal is not to find the "exotic" but to *de*-exoticize and find the emotional common ground throughout the world.

I view nearly all of the artists we work with as unsung (pun intended) heroes and strive to present them in as transparent and unvarnished a way as possible—to let the sounds and the singers stand on their own.

The majority of dismal and vacant records ever made feature pristine sound, while many classics sound like shit. The highest sound-to-truth ratio, emotion uncrowded by affectations stands the test of time—letting life comes as close as possible to speaking for itself.

I no more expect art from "artists" than moral guidance from Catholic priests.

Digital music making dissociates us from the primal—no matter how hard we hit a keyboard, the same sound results. Physicality is no longer a factor. Many records are now made without generating a single sound ever touching air and actually existing outside of the machine. Instead, the records solely contain remanipulated data.

Increasingly, music is created as an act of conformity—designed for computer program comprehensibility more than human emotion and sensual need.

The advances in computational technologies have allowed data to drive everything—reconfiguring music a left-brain versus right-brain creative activity.

But sound is nomadic by nature.

Often the assumed influences on a group are mistaken. Instead, influences are generally filtered through secondary or even tertiary sources: Tinariwen, listening to already diluted springs like Santana—hippies who poured a little LSD on the Blues and acted as if they'd changed the world. The Good Ones trio from Rwanda, learning songs from an Italian songbook donated by missionaries rather than at the knee of a local elder.

Personally, the first stranger to make my child laugh was a dead man, hamming it up in a post–World War II Italian B movie.

When we turn a sound around, it seems to last longer. The decay is slower and builds to something that fixes our attention. A transient attack instantly attracts us but past its peak is then dismissed just as abruptly since it already has "happened."

We live in a 95 percent mute world. The majority of objects we see emanate no discernible sound.

For decades, people have listened most intently to simulated and doctored sounds—multitrack recordings of events that never occurred and cinema soundtrack foley of sensationalized and reinforced noises. One of the secondary traumas of many mass-shooting survivors is how the sound was nothing like movie depictions. Instead, the gunshots rang deadly yet tinny and toylike, making the tragedy all the more disorienting due to its mismatch with what they'd expected.

We gorge daily on audio fictions.

Contrarians reflexively defend Autotune's ubiquitous use as an effect, but what they miss is that it is the Autotune that they *can't* hear—its airbrushing impact—that is so restrictive and concerning. It acts as cosmetic surgery for the voice. Subtler and invisible forces often prove the most dangerous.

A voice contains the weight of everything a person has and has not said. And whether intentional or not, vocal sounds possess the ability to enhance or undermine the meaning of what is stated.

If you slow down any speech enough and hold out the tone, it becomes singing. It becomes music. Pitch itself can only do one of three things—go up, down, or stay the same, but within those limitations infinity resides.

Interpersonal communications act as serenades.

As important as cross-cultural considerations are, they're not necessarily always as challenging as made out to be. Through the Esperanto of music, I've frequently found more in common with far-flung musicians throughout the world than with my next-door neighbors, family members, and fellow countrymen.

The aim is not cross-cultural collaboration, but *transcendence*—to achieve genuine human-to-human connection.

a music
manifesto
in fifty-
nine notes

Aesthetic Pitfalls

1.

Inequality itself not only leads to violence. It is violence.

2.

All people are musical. Music—like good and evil—inhabits every individual and exists on a continuum. Far from proprietary, pitch is in fact required to speak and rhythm to move.

Contrastingly, most people that claim to be musicians more precisely mean that they are simply instrument *owners*. They "play music" but often quite *un*-musically.

Unlike binary equations, culture and ability are always a matter of proportions. The question is not whether someone is musical/nonmusical. but to what degree various elements are prominent *and* consistent.

3.

Every baby is born with the potential to vocally produce *every* sound used in every language on earth. Therefore, to commit to and learn a mother tongue, a person must become less musical—developing certain muscles while allowing others to atrophy.

4.

Fretted and keyed instruments restricted musicality to right and wrong, either/or, on and off.

5.

Written sheet music divided people into musical and non-musical, literate and nonliterate.

6.

The commercialization of music led to divorcing it from daily life—reducing it to something obtained for a price, and only at sanctioned places and times.

7.

Recording converted music from an activity into an object that could be packaged and sold—a mutation from an inimitable, lived moment into a phantom that could be summoned at will.

Mass media led to the domination of single voices— reaching more people in seconds via a single radio performance or recording than otherwise could be tapped across a lifetime.

8.

Video transformed music into a predominantly visual experience. People began to listen with their eyes instead of their ears and developed greater self-consciousness as to how their choosing to support certain music made *them* look.

9.

Music is potentially the most democratic art form—invisible, blind taste tests of sound. Instead, it has become branded visually and the source has superseded the result. Audiences generally care more about who someone *is* than what they actually do. Who is saying something has come to dominate what is actually being said.

The result is superficially more diverse origins, but increasingly homogenized and undifferentiated results—listening with the eyes rather than the ears to music that *looks* different but sounds the same.

Proving that crappy and vacuous music can come from anywhere is far from a revolution.

Instead, more diverse distribution of inequality simply serves as decoy for true equality.

10.

Digital technology rendered music ethereal again—unlocking it from its plastic prisons. But paradoxically, digital technology only escalated music's objectification. It became something attained for free, to be trashed at will.

11.

In order for the audience members to deal with sorting through the sheer volume of cultural material, celebrity becomes the default—the rich get richer and the content more impoverished.

Thus an access-ocracy has been built.

12.

The crisis created by an access-ocracy is not whether a blessed birth person has talent. It is whether their talent is so much greater than less fortunate others that they are more deserving of attention.

The privileged person being "pretty good" or "not so bad" becomes a justification for not searching for other healthier and more enriching artists. This parallels the same trap that keeps people in other dysfunctional and addictive relationships.

Competition can reap benefits, but only when the rules are fair and the game not fixed from the start.

13.

Art theorists and critics obsessed with ancestral lineage act as cultural eugenicists, determining worth by bloodlines—their pedigree—instead of individuals. They treat artistry as if it can be bred like racehorses.

In doing so, well-worn but superficially explored assumptions slyly or unwittingly perpetuate racist ideology—that culture is engrained in DNA rather than shaped by distinct personalities and their interaction with and self-specific interpretations of their immediate environment.

14.

In a just system, every country would not only have a voice in popular media but *voices*.

Too often there is an assumption of fidelity for "foreign" cultures, a denial of the diversity and conflict contained within each. What is lost to outsiders is the accent *within the accent*.

Narratives should be told more by choir than solos.

15.

Lack of diversity leads to cultural inbreeding versus genetic fitness.

In all areas—nutrition, heredity, neurology—the wider the intake, the healthier the outcome.

16.

The star system at its core is an organizational one. The standardization it creates allows more money to be made from fewer people by promoting the false belief that the chosen ones are radically superior to a more varied field of producers.

17.

The standardization of measurements that made globalization of physical goods possible during post–World War II globalization has led also to a death knell in cultural variety. We have rapidly gone from the tuning of instruments varying from one neighboring village to another—and even from family to family—to the entire planet Autotuning on a matching grid to the same pitches.

18.

Technology has always enabled colonialization. In the past, it was the revolution of steel swords and armor, today cellphones and satellites.

When industrial powers ran out of land to conquer, they turned toward colonizing attention and time. Corporations claimstake words, phrases, and even color schemes, stealing available cognitive and expressive space.

Audiences consume "free" content by trading the most expensive resource—their own existence—and embrace art that robs more than stimulates imagination.

America no longer needs standing armies overseas. English-language media has conquered—annexing territory and occupying households around the globe.

19.

Digital-era records not only lack diversity in terms of age, gender, and culture but also sonically. The dynamics have been squashed to all peaks, little valley. The result: nominal contrast, an unnaturally narrow range in volume.

Yet the albums that have historically gained the most longevity (e.g., *Dark Side of the Moon* charting for 957 weeks since its release in 1973) almost invariably contain extraordinary dynamic range, nearly double that of the average record made today. Those classics take a journey and allow the ear to rest—to listen to the noises within the "quiet."

Worsening this trend of confinement, streaming services automatically "normalize" files so that every song is reproduced at the same volume, generating conformity via algorithms.

In order to create easily sharable digital files, massive amounts of sonic material must be excluded. What we are left with are skeletal sketches that shrink the spectrum, leaving holes and only enough information for us to complete the auditory illusion. The math is clear—if elements are being taken away, there is something lost regardless of whether we are cognizant of it or not.

Digital forces have ruthlessly downsized perception, concentrating only on those frequencies that can register consciously. They trash the rest, creating a vacuum. Analog also does not contain *all* sound, but features continuity across the spectrum, the same as is experienced in the natural world—without voids deliberately notched out.

20.

As the collective cultural momentum of the twentieth century stagnated, musical forms began to be identified through hyphenation and not unique naming. From that point forward, most creativity became founded on consumption versus idiosyncratic inspiration.

Culturally we contend with two compounding forces—societal norms and expectations shifting more rapidly, and people living longer, thus being forced to adjust to more change during a lifetime.

21.

A great lie of consumerism is that all output is dependent on input (i.e., influences) and that intrinsic and random elements cannot exist or prevail as factors.

This defies that nearly all musical revolutionaries—Coltrane, Fela, James Brown, Nina Simone, Billie Holiday, Hank Williams, Jimi Hendrix, Woody Guthrie—descended from nonmusical families.

Inspiration and singular insight remains one of the few things that money can't buy. Art results not from what we use, but how it is used. What matters is not where you're from or what you've been prescribed, but how much you learn from whatever you've been exposed to.

Sustainable, energy-efficient art makes more from few resources versus producing little—or worse, mere redundancy—from excess.

22.

Capitalism co-opts surfaces, emptying forms of their original content. The remaining subtext is that nothing really has significance except in service of the market.

Today, personal oddities, sexual orientation, and tragedy have been foregrounded as smokescreens adding spice to bland music. This is the polarity of the past where stars' scandals were instead closeted, muted, and denied.

23.

The barely veiled message of all mass media is there is no meaning at all. Constant cycles of misinformation and counterinformation generate cynicism and depression with the only prescribed and readily available remedy being evermore consumption.

The world is remade daily by these weapons of mass distraction.

24.

The most political music is the least obviously so. Its absence of meaning is more influential than any explicit diatribe. Triteness acts hypnotically as a Trojan Horse, bypassing the critical mind.

25.

With the professed legal abolition of prejudice in the post–civil rights era, capitalism was then free to institute an even more divisive and cynical structure: every person for themselves, all against all.

Ironically, the Left in particular is plagued by proprietorship—the drive to own ideas versus reach solutions collectively. Liberalism most often dies from "friendly fire."

26.

Pop music was a revolt: providing the underclass a large voice culturally. But by the 1970s, this uprising had been co-opted by corporations and converted into the advertising matrix—it was first sold *and* then used to sell *other*, completely unrelated goods—most of all, capitalism itself.

Corporations cannibalize our senses with the first act of violence to dull the imagination, denying options.

27.

The ultimate triumph of capitalism is to sell people con-
tentless content. The act of branding itself campaigns
to persuade people to purchase arbitrary symbols—what
something proposes to be versus what it actually is.

With products devoid of substance (or worse contain-
ing damaging elements like guns and alcohol), manufac-
turers are enabled to sell image instead: how the brand is
alleged to make you feel (a "Kool" cigarette), rather than
what it is. Mere emblems.

Laundry soaps are recast as sexy and loyalty pledged
to brands that promise to help you be "you." But in fact
wearing such logos and company uniforms, diminishes
rather than enhances our individuation.

The core goal of capitalism is to create surplus.
Resultantly, most citizens have now been made obsolete.
So the remaining solution is to anesthetize them with for-
mulaic content.

28.

Corporations are not immoral but amoral. They will produce whatever sells. But most of all what they are selling is planned obsolescence and change, the perpetually fake promise of fulfillment.

For if consumers were ever completely satiated, the compulsive need to buy would recede.

29.

Genre performers in essence produce nothing. The net result of their route repetition is a hollow occupation of space. Nothing new has resulted, only copycat clutter.

Art should not be judged on "quality" as much as impact—its ability to disrupt perception and generate memory beyond itself.

30.

Most art in the modern day is competing against quantity versus quality. As the population swells, the idea that "the cream will always rise to the top" has never been less true than now.

Over one hundred thousand records are released annually in the United States alone. That amount of content would require a person's every hour—including going without sleep entirely—if they were to listen to it all. It is literally impossible for everything commercially available to be heard, and it is revealing that over 20 percent of the songs posted on Spotify have reportedly never been streamed even once.

31.

One of the grand coups of capitalism is to label the arts as impractical. In fact, the arts are among the most practical pillars of education—they embody culture, help hone emotional intelligence, and provide a tangible, sharable experience of history.

Not even remotely an impractical thing to study, art is indispensable. It acts as societal ballast. Art serves as the cultural connective tissue.

32.

Consumerism transfigures creativity into a competitive act versus a cooperative endeavor, corrupting it with contact sports analogies. Tellingly, most digital-era pop stars now have business "teams," but exist without a single full-time band member.

It's fitting that music has ended up in football stadiums and hockey arenas, because it has been churned into acrobatics—a gesticulatory bloodbath. Without ever having been to one of artist _____'s concerts, one already knows the sequences and karaoke spectacle by heart.

If you cannot see the faces of the people that are performing and instead require a screen, it is not live, but *relayed* music.

33.

Commercial performers are concerned most with product versus process. Artists instead, explore the unknown and pursue truths that can only be uncovered through creative action.

Commercialized musicians preoccupy themselves with an imaginary (and usually adulatory) audience. Contrastingly, true artists sing to one specific person only—often themselves—knowing if they can reach them, they can reach the world.

34.

Recording divorced the labor from the artist. This severing allowed a level of capitalization never before possible in *any* industry—the ability to profit from individual effort even after someone's death, rendering their person ultimately dispensable.

35.

Art at its purest is differentiated from other products and creative pursuits by art's being pursued for its own intrinsic value.

Art has no utilitarian byproduct—it cannot be eaten or shelter someone physically. It leaves no material artifact that serves any pragmatic purpose beyond the emotional reaction it can evoke and its ability to potentially transform an environment aesthetically.

36.

Through the proliferation of mediocrity, fame has been fashioned more fascinating for the masses. The lowered bar of sheer luck, fate, and connections versus talent or dedication, places the illusion of stardom within reach of the hoi polloi.

Following the advent of cinema, radio, and television, citizens of the commercialized world consumed and internalized media content escalatingly until finally with social media they *became* the content. Consequently, the majority of interactions transmogrified into performative and transactional ones.

Moreover, tech titans centralized all needs to a single handheld device, clinching user's complete dependency. And with the inclusion of an alarm clock, it was all but dictated that one's personal phone would become the first thing most people touch in the morning, before even kissing their loved ones.

37.

Few people over the age of twelve want to passively listen to pop stars. We simply aren't allowed *not* to in most public spaces. They are imposed involuntarily, almost as a bureaucratic rite.

Media-saturated environments subject almost everyone compulsorily to the same information and songs. Few actively *choose* to listen to Drake or Ariana Grande, but nearly everyone has heard them, whether they are aware of it or not.

Mass media acts as mass hypnosis. If Nick Drake, Lorraine Ellison, and Big Star had been broadcast as tirelessly as the Beatles, more people would likely consider them indispensable as well.

38.

In manufacturing, the goal is to fabricate products with as few parts as possible—design a chair made with three elements instead of four, and profits soar.

Similarly, a manufacturer's goal is to sell fewer things but more of them. And with digital distribution's post-physicality, the sonic stock never runs out.

By nature capitalists monopolize and force their products into every available outlet—corn syrup and petroleum displace healthier ingredients, infusing almost everything. Correspondingly, lackluster music is piped into every possible electronic nook and cranny.

39.

No matter how antisocial the posture, hero worship is among the least rebellious acts possible.

Identity politics and celebrity are often poised as opposites, but in actually, they are intimately linked. Celebrity validates the inflated self-importance of individuals versus our commonality. Both help champion relativistic rationalizations as the norm, elevating the source of an opinion over the content of their ideas.

Yet timeless art's greatest power is its ability to function anonymously with no reduction of impact.

40.

Most pop artists trade in caricatures of nonconformity, serving as front-people for capitalism. Pop culture smuggles cynical ideation in as contraband.

41.

Success leads to an increase in confidence that can empower creativity. But there quickly comes a point where that same success generates arrogance and entitlement. At that very juncture, the creative ability that brought the success itself is diminished or destroyed.

What any one person has to contribute expressively can occur at any stage of life—during their teens, fifties, even toward the last moments of their lifetime. But once that core impulse is manifested to its fullest, it can rarely be surpassed by that same individual, and repeated attempts become paler versions of themselves.

The deadly shift is from artist to performer. As someone becomes "better" and more professional, their voice usually loses the edge and texture that first stimulated interest.

And over time they become tribute bands to themselves.

Some of the strongest songs ever written were by people *failing* to effectively copy another tune. This accidental ineptitude—versus exceptional vision or inspiration—was their strength. As they grow in technical prowess, they are able to duplicate more faithfully—becoming craftspeople—and consequently, whatever originality they possessed vanishes or is subsumed.

42.

The distinction between the career arc of veteran jazz musicians and pop stars is that the jazz artists venture fearlessly deeper into deconstructing the music as they aged, whereas pop artists circle around the same simplicity—fetishizing their own idiot savant-*ness*—hoping to rekindle that single, youthful flash of isolated genius which by design is ephemeral and elusive, rarely visiting someone more than once in a lifetime.

43.

Due to the spiritual power they possessed over fans, musicians rode the avant-garde of merchandizing. They were the first to cynically convert audiences into advertisers, their loyalists willing to not only offer up their own bodies—chests and foreheads—as billboards for the band's brand, but to even *pay* for the privilege to do so.

Artistic Guideposts

44.

Art is not only an empathy building device but also a short-cut. From one song or line, we can extrapolate entire universes of understanding and even achieve epiphanies.

Every reading, a resurrection, stories are often an act of suicide prevention.

45.

Specificity is the key to universality. Paradoxically, people can often better understand elements that are unfamiliar but that a given artist knows most intimately. Through detail, we are able to infer and translate another's experience to our own existence.

46.

All communication must cross three hurdles:

a) to hear what has been conveyed
b) to understand the message
c) to believe that it is true

Routinely, there is a presumed exactitude occurring within foreign translations. Yet, no matter what the language, people misunderstand each other with staggering frequency.

47.

Emotions exist not in isolation but as blends. They are rarely monochromatic experiences.

For example, when a parent passes, we are well aware that the prescribed feeling is sadness. But in reality, an entire spectrum of emotion is experienced. The sadness may be layered with fear, anger, gratitude, and relief, as well as guilt for having felt relieved at all.

Immature singers perform happy songs as if they are *only* happy. Underdeveloped actors portray anger exclusively with clenched fists, grimaces, and growls.

48.

Maturity in art is most commonly demonstrated by restraint—a willingness to use negative space and contrast. This is the opposite of a toddler's urge to fill an entire page with a single color, not leaving one inch unoccupied.

49.

The point of punk rock was not that anyone could be a star but that there should be *no* stars at all.

50.

Anytime someone must be elevated physically to be seen, then the space is too large for a direct interpersonal musical experience. Whenever there is division or barrier between spectators and performers, the music is no longer being made at human scale.

51.

In art, the middle ground is the danger. The gulf between "first thought, best thought" and belabored masterpieces is the no man's land where most commercialized entertainment flounders.

52.

Empathic responses are often invested disproportionately toward the wrong people. Instead, the more successful a performer has become, the greater scrutiny that they should face. If they cannot top themselves, then they should simply stop—or at least suspend—their output, posthaste and without excuses.

Too often, the famous are given a pass. The perennial comeback or return to form promo-narratives usually translate in actuality to new records that "don't suck *that* bad." These genuflections to mediocrity are precisely what makes most corporate media so dangerous—not its hideousness but its very banality. This is what allows it to be just palatable enough for the masses to remain passive in their consumption and not revolt.

As referenced earlier, this is the same phenomenon that keeps people trapped in abusive relationships—the concession that someone "isn't *that* bad." The fact that even the most hateful individuals possess *some* selectively redeeming qualities—no matter how deficient and dim— becomes a distorted justification for continued investment in them, regardless how destructive the net effect of that continued contact.

53.

The commercialized promotion of art trades in absolutes and hyperbolic communication. But ironically, art itself requires the courageousness to face ambiguity and embrace complexity—to confront and even celebrate nonbinary solutions and equations.

The antidote to damning or idealizing the world through generalized and exaggerated labels is to describe discrete actions in detail. For example, "He was throwing plates and screaming violently," not, "He *is* a violent person."

54.

The West's puritanical history compels us to pursue perfection. This drive interrupts creative momentum, corrupting the creative process toward conforming with external expectations rather than the quest to convey inner truth.

55.

A primary reason that modern music has lost spirituality is that computerized auto-correction tools fix the very places where the humanity is found—in the "mistakes"—the flat or sharp notes or rhythmic variance that spawn individuality and are evidence of difference.

56.

Historically, encores were not a call to play something new but to repeat the same song, delivered differently and even more powerfully—to push an artist further and make possible the experience of mutual surprise between audience and performer. These were moments that could not have occurred except in that precise moment and exact relationship.

Music played without risk—performed "live" with the guide rails and training wheels of click tracks and prerecorded vocal layers—lacks tension. Audiences may go home happy, but has anything shifted in their soul?

If you do not feel differently after a three-minute song has ended, then it has failed as art and functions instead only as entertainment. If one already knows how a story will turn or resolve and what the next notes of a melody or lines of a stanza will be, then the work is anesthetizing, not enlivening.

Most commercial songs and arrangements operate like laugh tracks, decreeing what and when to feel.

Nonetheless, expressiveness being demanding or weird for its own sake is just as one-dimensional and disingenuous. What's sought instead is concentrated communicative power, no matter how minimal the elements.

Though art forms should cultivate and treasure unpredictability, aesthetic ingenuity must also bear its own sense of logic and inevitability, no matter how intuitively or unintentionally divined.

57.

If art were strictly an intellectual process then every semi-competent film critic could rival Scorsese.

Academics know the words but not the tune, so to speak.

The issue is not whether someone is "smart." It is what they use their intellect for: courageous insight to know themselves better or the reflexive urge to build ever-escalating defense mechanisms for their ego, remaining emotionally arrested no matter how advanced their chronological age.

58.

Art is that which has reached the boiling point. It can be felt. Past that plateau, competition dissolves into sheer transcendence.

Finding freedom beyond form, creation in the moment eclipses the self to expand one's own soul.

Authentically generated sounds are as distinct as fingerprints.

Rock stars serve as hedonistic priests, engaging in accidental witchcraft. With the greatest musicians, every sinew of their being is given in service to the song.

59.

Expanding our ears to welcome more diverse and dissonant tones is to practice tolerance and actively develop a less judgmental view of our world.

It is not that we necessarily love a family member more than others, it is that we have little choice but to know them better. More intimacy and less division leads to greater empathy and understanding, and so it also follows when applied to strangers.

Art extends the bounds of family.

Mass Media Detox

1) Force oneself to listen to at least one thing daily that you've never heard before.
   a) If a song is challenging rather than easily accessible, recommit to giving it your full attention at least one more time.

2) Listen with the intention of understanding what a piece of music is attempting to communicate versus judging if it is good or bad.
   a) Tune in to whether someone is singing in an effort to make human connection or for self-glorification.

3) When faced with two near-equal works of art, *always* support the one from the less-represented perspective and background.

4)   Hold successful artists to a higher level of scrutiny, not a lower one, when they make demands on our attention.

5)   Refuse to celebrate music as a contrarian or ironic act, instead devote our limited energies solely to that which moves us most profoundly—physically or emotionally.
   a)   Robustly reject responsibility for metabolizing corporate media's glut and waste.

6)   As an act of liberation and purification of intent, every person should at least once write a song to the best of their ability, record it, listen back once, and then erase it *forever*.

Road Maps

Mmadi seeks shelter in one of the abandoned cars that seemingly outnumber the functioning ones on Grande Comore island.

Comoros:
We Are an Island,
but We're Not Alone

It took us six flights to reach the tiny African island, well sequestered in the Indian Ocean, and uninhabited by man until centuries *after* Christ.

Instead of sustenance farmers, here are found canoe boat sustenance *fishermen*. For them, the water is just a different kind of land. Regarded by locals as the lowest-class, that they haul in lobster for their families seems to take a bit of the edge off of the discontent and despair we have seen elsewhere such as in Malawi where some are forced to eat mice.

There is a trash-filled beach meters past the Presidential Palace, abutting its walls. The island's tone is so laid-back that when we performed a three-point turn in his driveway, it was without incident, barely detecting notice.

Just because we don't know an empire's history doesn't mean *they* don't know their history. (Every place is the center of the earth for those that live there. Most confuse their own civilization with *being* "civilization.")

Shortly after arriving, we inquired about the *ndzu-mara* (a double-reed pipe or primitive oboe), and were sadly informed, "*He* died." The last living player had just passed, the sound of the instrument ostensibly lost with him forever—reduced to having become synonymous with a single human life. We were only left to imagine the instrument's resonance.

The elders lamented that today the young people would rather buy than build instruments.

We'd hazarded a thirty-mile drive on the main road that took three hours each way due to the potholes, and even experienced a head-on collision as we stood stopped in the rain. A teenage driver with faulty brakes careened into our lane and then into us. Not having a seatbelt on, he was carried away—limp and unconscious—and his car then clumsily pushed to the side with nonchalance, so that sole transit artery could be reopened posthaste.

When we finally reached our destination, an elderly trio of mandolin, *oud*, and violin, were accompanied by a drummer who played his snare upside-down before being instructed otherwise by his compatriots. But as hospitable and regal as the group were, their watered-down *Tarab* music seemed half-baked.

Often, visitors demand a depth of cultural insight from "foreigners" that is naive and unwarranted. What's missed is that myopia and clueless people are to be found everywhere.

When searching for music, often the stronger artist is hidden behind another, more famous, but lesser one.

In this case, a slick and successful man named Hassain led us to another *non*-musician named Hassain who connected us with a musician who was quite good and it was he that ultimately introduced us to his friend and mentor. That person, Soubi (and his partner, Mmadi) turned out, at last, to be the real deal.

This mirrored almost exactly the process that we experienced with the Good Ones in Rwanda when we first recorded them in 2009. A quite passable singer recommended his teacher who then referred us to another singer who then insisted on delaying our recording a day in order to involve another band member. The end result was and remains magical.

The Comorian artists arranged for us to meet in an abandoned movie palace with sixty-foot-high ceilings and flying fox bats hanging upside-down from the rafters. Since the electricity was cut, the only light was from an open side-door leading to a lot that served as garbage dump and de facto community urinal, steps from the main street.

Snaking through the narrow alleys, it struck me how urban "slums" develop in much the same way as "charming" ancient Italian villages did—pedestrian streets laid out without a grid, built on top of each other ad hoc.

The musicians took turns playing a handmade, double-sided eight-string zither, simultaneously plucking both sides masterfully. Also, an eight-string, longnecked lute was tried.

But the sonic snag there was that the resulting sound was overly boomy due to the cavernous room. We tried pulling closed the dusty stage curtains to create some isolation, but what might have been a great environment to capture a huge trap kit or choir, for these two acoustic, solo performers left an aftertaste that was less than suitable.

And so, we reconvened the next day for another go.

The artist wanted to record "anywhere" but his own home. It is difficult to calculate how undesirable that locale may be, since the alternative was a seven-by-eight-foot metal shack with a rawboned foam mattress on the dirt floor as the only furnishing.

As he played, we dueled intermittently with construction workers next door who repeatedly agreed to stop hammering temporarily, but then would resume, as soon as we'd turned to walk away.

Worse, a tropical downpour began. Of all of the hazards of onsite recording, the most treacherous (aside from wind) is rain. Especially, if you are positioned beneath a tin roof. It creates a floor of white noise that ironically sounds nothing like rain since it is so lacking in definition. Divorced from context, ironically, a specific sound is often not "credible" in its purest form—nature rarely sounds like itself when reproduced. Thus film sound-designers tend to create foley from unrelated sources as stand-ins (e.g., crumpling cellophane to simulate a campfire; clacking coconut shells together for galloping horse hooves).

Kneeling on the dirt floor and encircled by mosquitoes, I killed one that splattered more blood across my neck than a slasher flick.

As so frequently occurs, the artist reserved his most melodically compelling song until the end—after we were broken down and departing, on the street, when at his most free. I'd defied one of my cardinal rules—never pack up the equipment until you're absolutely certain that the music is in fact finished.

I was left little choice but to stand in the rain holding a miniature backup device and try to capture this beautiful moment, both of us being drenched in the process. Counterintuitively, being amidst the rain provided superior sonics to being sheltered. But unfortunately, the moisture killed the machine and what was a resplendent take, was lost for eternity—witnessed only by me and a neighbor who stood bemused and finishing a cigarette in his doorway.

The few roads on the main island are lined with cars stripped of all but the body—car carcasses reclaimed by plant life. There seem more abandoned vehicles than those in use.

"Like Rwanda before the genocide," a survivor in Kigali later remarked.

With nowhere else to go, we opted for the partial shelter that one of these auto's shells provided from the coastal winds. It was a case of inverting the "listen to a final mix in your car" method of providing a real-life reference point, to instead simply starting the entire process there.

An additional bonus was the frame of the car acted as a microphone stand and resonator. We wedged a vocal mic between the roof and door frame, while a "room mic" was laid on the floor.

As is often the circumstance with outdoor and public recording, the sonics were highly dynamic due to the onlookers that tend to congregate, with increasing intensity the longer the recording progresses. So what may have started as a relatively noise-free environment can quickly turn into a landmine of whispers, distant greetings, well-intended but unhelpful hushings, throat clearings and coughs, and overly careful footsteps. That and cellphone's rings, vibrations, and signal interferences.

As Mmadi played a haunting tale of his friends perishing at sea while trying to emigrate, a small boy circled him distractedly. His steps were flanged by the lava rock beneath, adding a foreboding to the music that no mere instrument could ever provide.

I am a firm believer in allowing the time and place bleed into the sound. Isolating sources, if recording in the open, seems a clear contradiction, and more so, an exercise in futility.

Live recording without overdubs is imbued with truth since you are hearing something that actually happened versus a multitrack, staggered simulation of what never occurred.

When sound arrives precolored, rather than trying to make something less of what it is, it should be turned up—way up—as opposed to being sanitized. Similarly, if a noise is interfering, the best solution is counterintuitive: to mic it.

In postproduction it is usually easier to take away frequencies than add. For it is difficult to enhance sonics that aren't already there to begin with.

It is the high frequencies that we hear most when someone leans in close to whisper. With proximity, the low end drops away, as does reflected sounds. That is why vocals drenched in reverb, actually distance listeners from the source. For a voice to truly be foregrounded, present, and intimate, it need be as dry as possible.

In contrast to the massive but fragile systems that mid-twentieth-century field-recording pioneers like Colin Turnbull and Henrietta Yurchencho were forced to use, the main complaint about the main recorder I now use—a unit that can be balanced in a person's palm—is that it's, ironically, *too* small, sporting dials and buttons unmanageable for most adult fingers.

That said, despite the liberation digital technology has offered, in most cases, all told I still find myself lugging over a hundred pounds of gear, when factoring in stands and cables.

We should harness whatever momentum we're given. It is a gift. Should a toddler ever end up onsite (whether random neighborhood children or a young lass dragged there by her crazy, music-producer father) rather than a scolding, give him or her a microphone to hold and point instead.

It's the surest way to shut 'em up.

Rwanda:
Please See That We Are
Not Forgotten,
That the Songs
Live beyond Us

Flying over Lake Victoria, its immensity makes Tahoe seem like a puddle, over a hundred times in size. During an hour long flight, we barely left its circumference except during take-off and landing.

Electricity arrives to rural areas long before indoor plumbing. It's a lot easier to hang and string wire cross-country, than lay pipe. Nonetheless, just because electricity can be connected, doesn't make it free.

Therefore, citizens are fed television before clean water. *These* are the real "village people."

But the only savages I've ever spotted in Rwanda, were NGO workers from the Silicon Valley, drunkenly taking over a bar and simulating anal sex, while bent uninvited over a local couple's table.

According to Google, my mother-in-law's hometown doesn't exist, nestled in the hills above Lake Kivu where the road and Rwanda end, and the Congo awaits on the other shore.

For those who live without instruments, songs must first pass the gray-matter test—taking root in the originator's brain and proving able to remain there before being given external life and infecting others.

Christmas night there was flooding in Rwanda. Over a dozen people were killed and scores of homes destroyed.

The Good Ones' voices entwine in a familial way found only with those that've spent a lifetime singing together.

Janvier's one-room hut ended up chest deep in muddy water. It was a bitter twist—living with no indoor plumbing but having your home flooded nonetheless. Venice's floods had stolen headlines for weeks prior and afterward. Yet no one in that case had died or ended-up homeless. Yet, Venice's plight was purportedly more significant internationally due to the city's glamour. Rwanda's larger disaster meanwhile failed to register a blip.

The following morning, Janvier and his family nonchalantly welcomed Marilena and me into their home as if nothing had happened, even though they'd been up all night battling the water. Then, Janvier traveled the two-hour ride onward with us to Adrien's remote, hilltop farm.

Self-pity is a luxury only the rich can afford.

Over 83 percent of Rwandans continue to live rurally. Upwardly mobile urban dwellers or first-generation émigrés from throughout the diaspora that want to cut the rural population out of the narrative are the new colonialists. Rather than invested in truth, they possess a propaganda agenda.

A slick, aristocratic expat from a nation two weeks' drive away speaks of "we" at a meeting in Hollywood and is met with only reverent nods by a roomful of people who've never stepped foot in Africa or if so, only on safari—more interested in gorillas and giraffes than people.

With the cash from their first USA tour, Adrien bought a cow and electricity for his home. And so as we were recording, we crossed a new obstacle: the cow had to be fed to stop it from squalling.

For accompaniment, found objects from the farm were used as instruments, including a ten-gallon full milk jug that rang surprisingly hollow when struck.

Adrien and his partner Janvier have been singing together since childhood and the dovetailing harmonies reflect the single-voice harmonies only found with familial singing groups like the Carter Family, the Jackson 5, the Staple Singers, and the Everly Brothers. The two men trade off high and low parts so frequently that is often near impossible to tell who is singing what. With the musicians rural and remote hilltop origins, the similarity to American bluegrass vocals is often eerie.

At this particular meeting, Adrien and Janvier played each song together for the first time. Yet, with only a minute or two discussion beforehand, they fell in so seamlessly that these maiden ventures were indistinguishable in ease from the stalwart songs they'd played for decades.

Repeatedly, journalists have described the Good Ones' music as "traditional." But this assumption is false. No one within Rwanda (or outside) writes songs like Adrien. His are the product of one incredibly unique individual, deepened by two lifelong friends' harmonies and their singular gifts.

More than an African artist, Adrien is foremost simply one of the greatest living acoustic songwriters in the world. Individuals cannot only reflect culture, but at best, transform it—bringing us one song closer to God.

Due to the massive numbers that perished in 1994, Rwanda experienced an inverted baby-boom generation, in this case created by murder, not birth. The disproportionate representation of those under the age of twenty-four has generated a seismic "youth culture" shift in Rwanda, much the same as in the USA after World War II or in post-revolution Iran.

Though the youngest child, my mother-in-law appears the eldest in the only surviving photo of her family. All her siblings having been killed, the orphaned nephews and nieces surround my mother-in-law, half her size.

The capital, Kigali, is a scenic and vibrant city awash in optimism and progress. Defying the horrific footage of corpses lining roads twenty-five years ago, today Kigali is far safer than most American cities. Nonetheless, on their first attempt, the Good Ones were recently denied visas to perform in the United States, no matter how highly recommended they'd come. The embassy seemed unaccustomed to entertaining middle-aged men from the countryside with threadbare shoes and zero English skills.

Yet some of the most literary songwriters I've ever met are illiterate.

In my experience, it is not that people "everywhere" in the world speak English but that they are the ones that they are the ones overseas speaking *to us*.

A stone's throw away, the private schooled, aristocratic teenage children of friends are trilingual (French, English, Mandarin) yet still unable to converse in the national language. They live as tourists within their own nation, occupying without integration.

Americans from the coastal states now flock to Rwanda, touting how secure it is. What's lost is the tentative peace and its price—racking up one of the highest incarceration rates in the world and requiring airport-level security checks to even enter a supermarket or your own hotel.

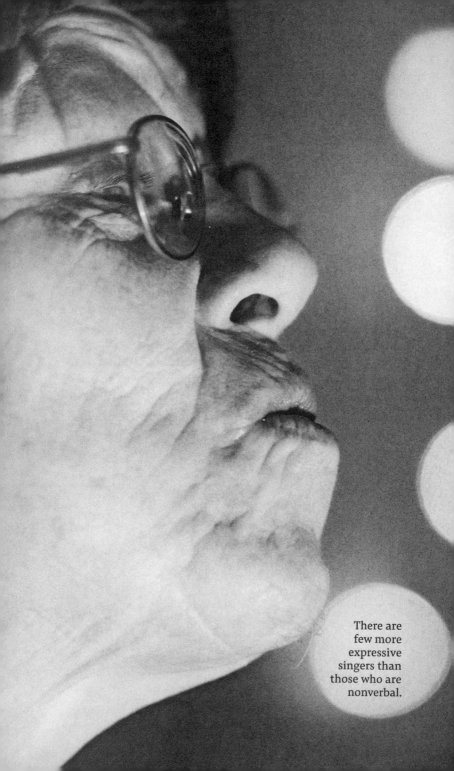

There are
few more
expressive
singers than
those who are
nonverbal.

Sheltered Workshop Singers: "Who You Calling 'Slow'?"

There are few more expressive singers than those that are nonverbal. Possessing a limited vocabulary dams up feelings, particularly when what few belabored words are uttered are not understood due to a speech impediment.

Miles east of the bay, in an aged strip mall tucked at the foot of the foothills' last stand before the enormity of the Central Valley, resides a weekday program for dozens of adults with varying cognitive and ambulatory abilities. Sharing a parking lot with a diner, liquor store, gaming shop, and sketchy massage parlor, the workshop employees occupy their weekday hours at the program.

Their diverse degrees of functioning were mirrored also in ego. No different from anywhere else, there were the self-acclaimed stars. And like elsewhere, those were the ones, whose voice's rang the least true.

A music expert recently asserted that at this stage of late capitalistic accumulation there are no "virgin births" left in music, that all is based on outside influence. This individual clearly has never witnessed what can happen when you hand a guitar for the first time to someone who has only partial use of their limbs.

We set up in a narrow, hollow-walled room with throbbing Technicolor lights and a disco ball, a place designed to have a paradoxically calming effect on some of the residents.

The instrumentation came from their immediate environment—a walker used as a bell, a yoga ball for a bass drum.

A diverse group of over twenty people participated in the project, ranging in age from twenties to sixties (with the life expectancy of their population being a mere sixty years old). Over half were women. Many were wheelchair users. None had sung before into a microphone or attempted a stringed instrument.

Though as a group they struggled to entrain with one another—be it choral singing or handclaps—many synched vocally without direction to other musical patterns around them, no matter how faint. They shaped melodies out of thin air, fitting their accompaniment.

My only sister was among the participants. Having pushed past fifty, her precipitous approach to the given life expectancy has begun to show in diminished orientation, expressiveness, and hearing.

Growing up, I'd seen my sister's discomfort—eyes steered down sideways and hard, unable to contain her oversized tongue due to the shame—too many times to not remain vigilant, playing defense for a lifetime. I inherited little choice but to side with those marginalized.

Many people stared and pointed. Others snickered or laughed. Some even hurled the r-word, the default slur: "retard." Whether under breath or out loud, it was the one trigger that could belie my sister's otherwise gentle and loving nature.

I grew up ready and braced for a fight. But the futility of those early failed fisticuffs dampened my rage with time until I ultimately succumbed to the sadness that lay beneath it all. Hate could not be overcome one individual at a time. In fact, personal confrontation only intensified those divisions. Hatred rose from a more indestructible and primitive source: fear.

Jane was caught between deinstitutionalization from state-run hospitals and the mainstreaming movement that gained traction in the 1990s and led to the integration of special needs students into standard classrooms. Hers instead was Generation X, literally, but also doubled within their own subculture.

Therefore, she was bussed to a segregated school—a kind of educational apartheid, with a campus for those with developmental disabilities on one side and physical disabilities on the other, sifted at the end of the same remote cul-de-sac.

She is clinically diagnosed as "severely retarded," just one step above the lowest denomination of catatonic and mute.

Our main connection was through music—joy expressed through dance, sadness and longing with melody. Jane taught me a different kind of listening. Not so much with the ears but the spirit, with your entire being.

My mother was often weighed down by her own mental health issues, unable to even rise from bed. As our family weathered the two-pronged assault of the Me decade and its resulting divorce explosion, it was often Jane that did the comforting. It was her that seemed the true caretaker.

When she was around eight years old Jane became obsessed with television personality, Tony Orlando, who had a weekly variety program which she'd watch as if hypnotized, her attention span stretching from a measure of minutes to an hour. Even then I couldn't understand the appeal. Only later did I discover where the connection may've laid. Orlando's only sister also had Down syndrome. Whenever he broke the fourth wall and directly addressed the camera—as he was wont to do—it was as if he and my own sister were exchanging some secret handshake through the screen, their histories intertwining.

The universal, but oft forgotten underdogs throughout the world are those who face disabilities. The prejudice against them is an almost inescapable inclination, traversing frontiers, permeating most cultures. Fortunately, those facing physical limitations have demanded and made tremendous progress in accessibility throughout the industrialized world during recent decades. But the developmentally and intellectually disabled are often left voiceless, due in large part to their often genetically impacted speech abilities.

One woman's only liability was her own prolificness. Grace reportedly spends hours a day, isolating and consoling herself with song. The self-serenades that stream from her seemed potentially endless. Such was the surplus that the only apparent artistic risk was stopping too soon. While beholding her ability, the limitations of the recording process were laid bare. We could only hope to catch the moment, but not the eternal place from which the music was born.

Proportions are what we should be concerned with. Yes, many with Down syndrome are kinder than most people, but I learned at a young age that some of them could act like assholes too. No one has a monopoly on goodness or ill.

This record is possibly my most personal work ever—even more than my repeated singer-songwriter misfires in the 1980s and 1990s. The recordings were made with the involvement of my father during his final stage battling cancer. We knew that if this long-envisioned collaboration was ever to happen, the time was nigh at hand. Sadly, my father passed just two months afterward.

One of the greatest surprises came from a man who was a classmate of my sister's since they were both toddlers, decades spent riding the short bus together for hours as it circled the valley daily collecting kids. Tom had always been a macho dude and a bit of an archetypal "bad boy," even pursuing bodybuilding as a teen. But the hurt that rose from deep inside his breast as he sang of his father was devastating.

Many of the most musical people in the world have never touched an instrument or dared open their mouths in song. They express it instead through movement or even just the manner with which they peer out into the world.

Knowing too well the sky-high rates of abuse that afflict their population, to hear a workshop artist sing of "bad memories," can only make one shudder and dare wonder to what interpersonal horrors he might refer.

If one wants to run a quick litmus test on the moral fitness of a society, look no further than how they treat their most vulnerable. It should never be disregarded that mentally ill and physically disabled hospital patients were exterminated by the Nazis, having been pronounced as possessing "life unworthy of life." This was the process that mushroomed to claim millions in extermination camps.

Immediately following the completion of the Sheltered Workshop recordings, I left for Italy but became stranded there due to the COVID-19 pandemic.

Just weeks after, my father began to fade and I organized Jane a ride over to see him one last time. The reunion took place just hours before he passed. Immediately after Jane's visit, the nurse said my father grew solemn and, after a few contemplative moments, began to transition from this life. There is a certain poetry in a daughter—who was sent home to die (at the doctor's direction) as a premature infant—being the one who fifty-five years later helped her father make peace with his own demise.

Decades on, the survivors of the Kosovo war
grapple with the consequences.

War Women of Kosovo:
A Lifetime Isn't
Long Enough

Almost as a counterweight to mustachioed military men in camouflage, kids outnumbered adults on the flight in, the average age hovering somewhere in single digits. The plane screamed its way into Pristina—a choir of cries.

Instead of military stripes, today the men on the streets bear Nike swipes.

When we told a family member we were traveling to Kosovo, their response was, "Isn't there a war there?"

A more correct response would be, "Isn't there war everywhere?"

Three decades on and tragedy remains the staple association for an entire nation, the economically poorest in Europe.

At the border, the COVID restrictions remained severe. But once we pulled clear of the airport, not a mask was seen. After enduring bombing, invasion, and foreign rule, a tendency toward noncompliance seemed almost a cultural necessity.

A minimum of eight hundred thousand out of fewer than two million citizens were made refugees during the Kosovo war—nearly half the country turned homeless, with women systematically subjected to rape by Serbian soldiers in what the UN tribunal later charged as genocide and crimes against humanity.

We traveled west to record with dozens of women who are provided with medical, psychological, and economic support by a Kosovan female run NGO. Only two of the participants had previously sung solo or written songs or poems before.

In a neighborhood cafe, the Blue-eyed Blues chiming overhead sounded deeper due to its being displaced. It still didn't sound particularly good, but nonetheless improved. In a region weighted with sadness, it's not difficult to see how wails from all comers resonate.

A UK music critic accused us of trying to anonymize the singers since they were identified only by initials. But it was the women who insisted for protection that their faces, names, and towns should not be made public.

Many of the women had never left their villages, even to visit the small city ten minutes' drive away.

We recorded in the house where one woman was raped while her husband was bound and gagged in the next room. This location was not chosen for dramatic effect, but simple necessity. It is where the couple have continued to live over the decades since. In fact, many survivors from the community still reside in the very houses where their parents were killed and they sexually assaulted. Worse, the majority were violated by not one but multiple assailants.

Quelling our fears that sharing their stories may reopen wounds, instead they recurrently stated, "We get strength from you listening to our stories. You give us courage."

In the telling of their tales, there often would be a phrase that would stick out for its sudden musicality—little melodic seismographic disturbances—amid what were otherwise monotones. When translated, these bits invariably carried the most acute lyrical and emotional meaning.

Around the corner, we stumbled upon a high school girl being bullied by a stocky boy, egged on by a mob of peers. He held her tightly by both wrists until we leaned on the horn. And then he gave chase. Certain heritages prove hard to shake.

My wife Marilena's only two living Rwanda relatives were born of genocidal rape. And at twenty-one, my life was knocked asunder following the sexual assault of a loved one. I attended the emotional gutting that can occur, how in minutes a person can be left a ghost. I learned trauma's reach—surging secondarily through the veins of family and friends, eventually being handed down to subsequent generations.

In Kosovo, as so sadly often is the case, the victims often suffer the retraumatization of being doubted or blamed, accused of manufacturing stories to qualify for government assistance. And those who cannot produce eyewitnesses to their assaults are left unassisted, a particularly chilling bureaucratic twist given how frequently their husbands and family members were present for and then murdered during these very incidents.

The horror stories that the women shared were chillingly similar. More than one was months pregnant when she was attacked. One said that the bond with her son was exceptionally strong, "because he was inside me when it happened and gave me strength." Another recounted her infant son being thrown from the bed, making room on the mattress to rape her.

Another survivor recited her story by rote at first. But when asked to sing it, she launched into an improvised melody of microtonal intricacy, and the stream of consciousness lyrics flowed out of her, bringing the therapist to tears.

"I cannot translate these words. *These* are too beautiful."

Time may heal all wounds. But with some injuries, a lifetime isn't long enough.

In the Malawi Mouse Boys' passage from boys to
men, two were left to fight COVID-19 alone.

Malawi Mouse Boys: Other Neighborhoods Just Have Better Publicists

The Malawi Mouse Boys were mocked online for using Coke can percussion. The trolls claimed that the band's doing so was a bid for "authenticity" and not out of necessity. This exemplifies how international bands are routinely put through a cynical, hipster filter.

Relatedly, a liberal rock star friend once boasted how he'd seen one of the Malawi Mouse Boys' first performances and marveled about how "awesome" they'd been. He persisted with this conviction despite my informing him that the band had never yet stepped foot in the United States and had only been on a stage *anywhere* a handful of times. Undeterred and unrepentant, in his memory, some other, unnamed "African" band served as surrogates.

When the Malawi Mouse men finally did tour California, we stopped to view the Elephant Seals lining the coastline and slowing traffic.

After observing countless tons of meat lining the ocean's edge, there was a pause and Joseph turned to me and asked, "Do you eat them?"

When I told him no, he replied with rare irritation.

"Why not?"

Understandably, when survival is at stake, conservationism takes a backseat if not getting ditched entirely.

Far from savior syndrome, I beheld the near riot triggered by gifting a soccer ball to kids in Zondiwe's village. The community's fabric was rent within minutes as the entire history of capitalism played out in tears and fists before our eyes.

A frequent refrain that Marilena and I hear throughout the world is "But I'm from _____," as if that alone grants some overriding aesthetic eye or entitlement. The equivalent would be me feeling fully licensed to rush the stage at a Beach Boys concert because I was raised in California (regardless of having never surfed in my life).

In 2020, just as Ferrari-driving rapper substitutes for poverty porn reached the continent full blown, COVID-19 hit. Preoccupied with its own concerns, the industrialized world turned its back even further on Africa. Commercialized Afrobeats star's from capital cities played right along, preaching Prosperity Gospel propaganda from their economic bubbles.

Representation should mean more than having shitty commercialized music resourced from every last outpost—diversity reduced to just one color: Green/Greed.

I'm haunted by the brutal and unjust degree to which the majority of my own "problems" remain so small that they aren't even really problems at all. It is not that as a straight, white male things for me are infinitely easy, but they are undeniably and unconscionably *easier* than for most overall.

Pakistan Is for
the Peaceful

Inexplicably, many people remain more afraid of Muslims praying than white men with guns.

One can easily name many accomplished artists that have been terrorized (Selena, Dimebag Darrell, the Miami Showband, and most infamously John Lennon were all assassinated by fans or associates), but not one that was themselves a terrorist. *If* an aspiring terrorist was ever even committed and patient enough to undertake deep cover by mastering a forty-nine-note scale, I'm certain that by the time they'd finished their training they would fundamentally be a changed person and no longer lust to launch such an attack.

Aside from one incident in South Sudan, the only person who ever tried to abduct me was an Uber driver in Austin, and the one occasion I've witnessed the immediate aftermath of someone murdered was in my birthplace, Oakland.

At age seventy-seven, Ustad Saami still practices from 4:00 a.m. to noon most days, drilling himself with exercises. Though his physical hearing has declined and he now requires in-ear aides for daily communication, his powers of perception continue to rise. Personally, as an antidote to ageism, I am invested in how voices mature.

As a child, he was the chosen one from his family and his master forbade him to speak for years. During this

Microtonal vocal master Ustad Saami tunes to a note few can hear.

period he was only allowed to express himself vocally, not verbally. He studied for thirty-five years to perfect this system before ever even undertaking a concert. His is the same trajectory as puff-pop stars like Justin Bieber and the ilk, only inverted—they start performing prematurely and get even more flaccid over time.

Amateurs and virtuosos share a similar freedom of expression. It is the hinterlands between the two—amateur and master—that mediocrity lies. And that is the bulk of the musicians heard through commercial channels.

Instead, Ustad explores the subtlety of human emotion through microtones, an attempt to turn "negatives positive" through the reclamation of the tones that have been designated disposable and out of tune.

Following Saami's recent debut album, a world music expert in Los Angeles was flummoxed that she could not find any reference to the master's system on the internet. His *"surti"* scale cannot be found elsewhere precisely because it is *his* system—a customized project of sonic recovery and inclusion—with Ustad the only living vocal practitioner.

In 2016, a popular singer, Amjad Sabri was assassinated not far from Ustad's home due to the Taliban believing Amjab's music "blasphemous." To the north, dozens of Sufi dancers have been killed and temples razed. But more than physical danger, what Ustad has faced is career jeopardization due to his refusing to conform to orthodoxy, both ideologically and musically.

By singing in disparate languages—including dead ones—he has made the ultimate anticommercial choice: to sing in words that have no land of their own, to perform songs whose lyrics are as unintelligible in his own country as would be Basque or Cantonese.

Epilogue

Railroad Song

My father worked the railroad his entire life, as did his grandfather after emigrating as an orphan from postfamine Ireland.

My great-grandfather claimed that the railroad's multicultural workforce had no choice but to find some common language. Across long distances, this was often crude arm motions and hand signs, their articulateness of life-and-death consequence.

It was along those same east-west tracks that freed (and *not freed*) African American slaves, Irish immigrants, and Civil War veterans had mingled in temporary tent boomtowns after having swung picks and sledgehammers side by side in the daylight—laying one tie at a time—while moving west as the Pawnee ran security detail. Eventually, the workers collided north of the Utah salt flats with Chinese laborers who'd made their way from California in a race to finish first.

Yet somehow the official group photo of this monumental meeting did not feature a single non-Caucasian face, save a lone Native American obscured and in shadow toward the back.

Throughout time, it has always been the travelers that have carried culture back with them. They are the "change agents"—the fishermen, soldiers, hunters, merchants, and troubadours.

Not surprisingly, many migratory singers write about the act of traveling itself and the Blues itself was a largely a celebration of this newfound, postslavery right. Later, it was with folk legend Woody Guthrie, leading the way that an entire body of hobo tunes entered popular culture from the fringes in the 1940s.

But just as important as the possibility for cultural transmission that train lines offered is what the machines themselves directly fueled.

First, they provided hope—that other prospects awaited beyond the horizon. However remote, they create a connection to tomorrow by way of unbroken, hand-laid tracks.

Second, through each of their very passages—whether bisecting a metropolis, a backwood town, or crossing state lines—trains infected North America with new rhythms. The gears and pistons were the percussion, the whistle the melody.

The human heartbeat acts as the nuclear metronome for all music. But it was the mechanized rhythms of trains that squired jazz into being—as well as accelerating that music's diffusion. A century later, V8 hot rods propelled rock 'n' roll's birth, followed by interspace rockets launching not just monkeys and satellites but unprecedented psychedelic sounds.

There would be no Jimi Hendrix without this trajectory.

In hard rock's wake, not only did New York subway trains and platforms provide a vital staging ground for prototypical rappers, breakdancers, and graffiti artists, but it is no mere coincidence that an elevated rail traversed the South Bronx neighborhood where hip-hop was born, the avenues below radiating with near-constant resonance.

My father had a one-inch scar just below his heart where he was stabbed as a teenager, a new hire on a railroad section gang. This occurred near Death Valley's southern border, fittingly enough. He never talked about what happened. I only heard tell of it secondhand. Even then, vague details existed. Apparently it was some sort of disagreement at mealtime fed to fists by my father's shoddy Spanish.

Framed in my hallway is a photo of my two-year-old father in front of a stencil-stamped iron horse. He is being held by his grandfather on the day of his retirement after decades on the job. My great-grandfather smiles, bedecked in that era's standard-issue uniform: denim overalls, bandana, and a railroad engineer cap.

During their careers, both men came to witness more than one death beneath their locomotive wheels—drunken men refusing to yield the track, instead using it as a balancing beam; automobiles bypassing crossing signs, sacrificing life in a race to save seconds.

My father was not musically inclined at all. Like most heterosexual males, his vocal expressions had been actively shut down. He resorted to whistling as the one acceptable outlet, often irritatingly looping snippets of hackneyed melodies for minutes.

When my sister and I were young, my father would take us some Saturday mornings to the railway switching yard in West Oakland where he worked. He would raise me up on his shoulders as passenger trains thundered by.

We'd wave as they passed, and hardly a person aboard failed to wave back, creating an unfurled string of greeting—their bodies and minds loosened by the motion, their spirits lifted by the purpose of a shared destination.

In its roar could be heard a song.

The author searches for freedom in the
voices of Zomba Prison's residents.

About the Author

Ian Brennan is a Grammy-winning music producer who has also produced three other Grammy-nominated albums. He is also the author of seven books and has worked with the likes of Fugazi, Merle Haggard, Tinariwen, and Green Day, among others. His work with international artists such as the Zomba Prison Project, Tanzania Albinism Collective, and Khmer Rouge Survivors, has been featured on the front page of the *New York Times* and on an Emmy-winning segment for the television program *60 Minutes* with Anderson Cooper reporting.

He also has taught violence prevention and conflict resolution around the world since 1993 for such prestigious organizations as the University of London, the New School (NYC), Berklee College of Music, the Smithsonian, Bellevue Hospital (NYC), the Betty Ford Clinic, UC Berkeley, and the National Academy of the Sciences (Rome).

Of Brennan's previous works, *Hi-Fi Choice* magazine stated, "It's not often that you read a book that changes the way you listen to music . . . if you only read one book about music this year, I strongly recommend that you make it this one," while *R2* magazine raved, "Beg, borrow, or buy a copy of this important book now." *Songlines* magazine called Brennan's writing "a thought-provoking read that challenges our preconceptions on almost every page."

About the Photographer

Marilena Umuhoza Delli is a Rwandan-Italian photographer, author, and filmmaker whose photographic work has been published around the world by the BBC, CNN, NPR, Al Jazeera, The Guardian, VICE, *Libération*, *Corriere della Sera*, *Le Monde*, *Rolling Stone*, *Smithsonian*, and the *New York Times*, among others. She has written two Italian-language books about racism and growing up with an immigrant mother in Italy's most redneck region.

She holds a master's degree in Language for International Communication for which she wrote her thesis on African cinema. Additionally, she studied filmmaking at the University of California, Los Angeles (UCLA).

ABOUT PM PRESS

PM Press is an independent, radical publisher
of books and media to educate, entertain, and
inspire. Founded in 2007 by a small group of
people with decades of publishing, media, and
organizing experience, PM Press amplifies the
voices of radical authors, artists, and activists.
Our aim is to deliver bold political ideas and vital stories to all walks
of life and arm the dreamers to demand the impossible. We have sold
millions of copies of our books, most often one at a time, face to face.
We're old enough to know what we're doing and young enough to know
what's at stake. Join us to create a better world.

PM Press
PO Box 23912
Oakland, CA 94623
www.pmpress.org

PM Press in Europe
europe@pmpress.org
www.pmpress.org.uk

FRIENDS OF PM PRESS

These are indisputably momentous times—the
financial system is melting down globally and
the Empire is stumbling. Now more than ever
there is a vital need for radical ideas.

In the years since its founding—and on a
mere shoestring—PM Press has risen to the formidable challenge
of publishing and distributing knowledge and entertainment for the
struggles ahead. With over 450 releases to date, we have published an
impressive and stimulating array of literature, art, music, politics, and
culture. Using every available medium, we've succeeded in connecting
those hungry for ideas and information to those putting them into
practice.

Friends of PM allows you to directly help impact, amplify, and revitalize
the discourse and actions of radical writers, filmmakers, and artists. It
provides us with a stable foundation from which we can build upon our
early successes and provides a much-needed subsidy for the materials
that can't necessarily pay their own way. You can help make that
happen—and receive every new title automatically delivered to your
door once a month—by joining as a Friend of PM Press. And, we'll throw
in a free T-shirt when you sign up.

Here are your options:

- **$30 a month** Get all books and pamphlets plus 50% discount on all
  webstore purchases

- **$40 a month** Get all PM Press releases (including CDs and DVDs)
  plus 50% discount on all webstore purchases

- **$100 a month** Superstar—Everything plus PM merchandise, free
  downloads, and 50% discount on all webstore purchases

For those who can't afford $30 or more a month, we have **Sustainer
Rates** at $15, $10 and $5. Sustainers get a free PM Press T-shirt and a
50% discount on all purchases from our website.

Your Visa or Mastercard will be billed once a month, until you tell us to
stop. Or until our efforts succeed in bringing the revolution around. Or
the financial meltdown of Capital makes plastic redundant. Whichever
comes first.

Silenced by Sound: The Music Meritocracy Myth

Ian Brennan
with a Foreword by Tunde
Adebimpe

ISBN: 978-1-62963-703-7
$20.00   256 pages

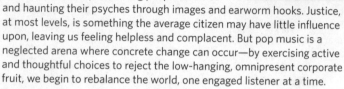

Popular culture has woven itself into the social
fabric of our lives, penetrating people's homes
and haunting their psyches through images and earworm hooks. Justice,
at most levels, is something the average citizen may have little influence
upon, leaving us feeling helpless and complacent. But pop music is a
neglected arena where concrete change can occur—by exercising active
and thoughtful choices to reject the low-hanging, omnipresent corporate
fruit, we begin to rebalance the world, one engaged listener at a time.

Silenced by Sound: The Music Meritocracy Myth is a powerful exploration
of the challenges facing art, music, and media in the digital era. With his
fifth book, producer, activist, and author Ian Brennan delves deep into his
personal story to address the inequity of distribution in the arts globally.
Brennan challenges music industry tycoons by skillfully demonstrating
that there are millions of talented people around the world far more
gifted than the superstars for whom billions of dollars are spent to
promote the delusion that they have been blessed with unique genius.

We are invited to accompany the author on his travels, finding and
recording music from some of the world's most marginalized peoples.
In the breathtaking range of this book, our preconceived notions of art
are challenged by musicians from South Sudan to Kosovo, as Brennan
lucidly details his experiences recording music by the Tanzania Albinism
Collective, the Zomba Prison Project, a "witch camp" in Ghana, the
Vietnamese war veterans of Hanoi Masters, the Malawi Mouse Boys,
the Canary Island whistlers, genocide survivors in both Cambodia and
Rwanda, and more.

Silenced by Sound is defined by muscular, terse, and poetic verse, and
a nonlinear format rife with how-to tips and anecdotes. The narrative
is driven and made corporeal via the author's ongoing field-recording
chronicles, his memoir-like reveries, and the striking photographs that
accompany these projects.

After reading it, you'll never hear quite the same again.

If It Sounds Good, It Is Good: Seeking Subversion, Transcendence, and Solace in America's Music

Richard Manning with a Foreword by Rick Bass

ISBN: 978-1-62963-792-1
Price: $26.95   320 pages

Music is fundamental to human existence, a cultural universal among all humans for all times. It is embedded in our evolution, encoded in our DNA, which is to say, essential to our survival. Academics in a variety of disciplines have considered this idea to devise explanations that Richard Manning, a lifelong journalist, finds hollow, arcane, incomplete, ivory-towered, and just plain wrong. He approaches the question from a wholly different angle, using his own guitar and banjo as instruments of discovery. In the process, he finds himself dancing in celebration of music rough and rowdy.

American roots music is not a product of an elite leisure class, as some academics contend, but of explosive creativity among slaves, hillbillies, field hands, drunks, slackers, and hucksters. Yet these people—poor, working people—built the foundations of jazz, gospel, blues, bluegrass, rock 'n' roll, and country music, an unparalleled burst of invention. This is the counterfactual to the academics' story. This is what tells us music is essential, but by pulling this thread, Manning takes us down a long, strange path, following music to deeper understandings of racism, slavery, inequality, meditation, addiction, the science of our brains, and ultimately to an enticing glimpse of pure religion.

Use this book to follow where his guitar leads. Ultimately it sings the American body, electric.

"Richard Manning is the most significant social critic in the northern Rockies. We're fortunate to have Dick Manning as he continues his demands for fairness while casting light on our future."
—William Kittredge, author of *The Last Best Place: A Montana Anthology* and *The Next Rodeo: New and Selected Essays*

"Richard Manning's work has always been something special, distinguished by its intense passion and its penetrating insights."
—George Black, author of *Empire of Shadows: The Epic Story of Yellowstone*

The Explosion of Deferred Dreams: Musical Renaissance and Social Revolution in San Francisco, 1965-1975

Mat Callahan

ISBN: 978-1-62963-231-5
$22.95   352 pages

As the fiftieth anniversary of the Summer of Love floods the media with debates and celebrations of music, political movements, "flower power," "acid rock," and "hippies", *The Explosion of Deferred Dreams* offers a critical re-examination of the interwoven political and musical happenings in San Francisco in the Sixties. Author, musician, and native San Franciscan Mat Callahan explores the dynamic links between the Black Panthers and Sly and the Family Stone, the United Farm Workers and Santana, the Indian Occupation of Alcatraz and the San Francisco Mime Troupe, and the New Left and the counterculture.

Callahan's meticulous, impassioned arguments both expose and reframe the political and social context for the San Francisco Sound and the vibrant subcultural uprisings with which it is associated. Using dozens of original interviews, primary sources, and personal experiences, the author shows how the intense interplay of artistic and political movements put San Francisco, briefly, in the forefront of a worldwide revolutionary upsurge.

A must-read for any musician, historian, or person who "was there" (or longed to have been), *The Explosion of Deferred Dreams* is substantive and provocative, inviting us to reinvigorate our historical sense-making of an era that assumes a mythic role in the contemporary American zeitgeist.

"Mat Callahan was a red diaper baby lucky to be attending a San Francisco high school during the 'Summer of Love.' He takes a studied approach, but with the eye of a revolutionary, describing the sociopolitical landscape that led to the explosion of popular music (rock, jazz, folk, R&B) coupled with the birth of several diverse radical movements during the golden 1965-1975 age of the Bay Area. Callahan comes at it from every angle imaginable (black power, anti-Vietnam War, the media, the New Left, feminism, sexual revolution—with the voice of authority backed up by interviews with those who lived it."
—Pat Thomas, author of *Listen, Whitey! The Sights and Sounds of Black Power 1965-1975*

One Chord Wonders: Power and Meaning in Punk Rock

Dave Laing
with a Foreword by TV Smith

ISBN: 978-1-62963-033-5
$17.95   224 pages

Originally published in 1985, *One Chord Wonders* was the first full-length study of the glory years of British punk rock. The book argues that one of punk's most significant political achievements was to expose the operations of power in the British entertainment industries as they were thrown into confusion by the sound and the fury of musicians and fans.

Through a detailed examination of the conditions under which punk emerged and then declined, Dave Laing develops a view of the music as both complex and contradictory. Special attention is paid to the relationship between punk and the music industry of the late 1970s, in particular the political economy of the independent record companies through which much of punk was distributed. The rise of punk is also linked to the febrile political atmosphere of Britain in the mid-1970s.

Using examples from a wide range of bands, individual chapters use the techniques of semiology to consider the radical approach to naming in punk (from Johnny Rotten to Poly Styrene), the instrumental and vocal sound of the music, and its visual images. Another section analyses the influence of British punk in Europe prior to the music's division into "real punk" and "post-punk" genres.

The concluding chapter critically examines various theoretical explanations of the punk phenomenon, including the class origins of its protagonists and the influential view that punk represented the latest in a line of British youth "subcultures." There is also a chronology of the punk era, plus discographies and a bibliography.

"A clear, unprejudiced account of a difficult subject."
—Jon Savage, author of *England's Dreaming*

Working-Class Heroes: A History of Struggle in Song: A Songbook

Edited by Mat Callahan and Yvonne Moore

ISBN: 978-1-62963-702-0
$14.95   96 pages

Working-Class Heroes is an organic melding of history, music, and politics that demonstrates with remarkably colorful evidence that workers everywhere will struggle to improve their conditions of life. And among them will be workers who share an insight: in order to better our lot, we must act collectively to change the world. This profusely illustrated treasury of song sheets, lyrics, photographs, histories, and biographical sketches explores the notion that our best hope lies in the capacity of ordinary working people to awaken to the need to emancipate ourselves and all of humanity.

Featuring over a dozen songwriters, from Joe Hill to Aunt Molly Jackson, *Working-Class Heroes* delivers a lyrical death blow to the falsehood that so-called political songs of the twentieth century were all written by intellectuals in New York. Many, like Ella May Wiggins, were murdered by the bosses. Others, like Sarah Ogan Gunning, watched their children starve to death and their husbands die of black lung, only to rise up singing against the system that caused so much misery.

Most of the songs collected here are from the early twentieth century, yet their striking relevance to current affairs invites us to explore the historical conditions that inspired their creation: systemic crisis, advancing fascism, and the threat of world war. In the face of violent terror, these working-class songwriters bravely stood up to fight oppression. Such courage is immortal, and the songs of such heroes can still lift our spirits, if we sing them today.

Featured in this twenty-song collection are Sarah Ogan Gunning, Ralph Chaplin, Woody Guthrie, Ella May Wiggins, Joe Hill, Paul Robeson, John Handcox, Aunt Molly Jackson, Jim Garland, Alfred Hayes, Joseph Brandon, and several anonymous proletarian songwriters whose names have been long forgotten, though their words will never die.

"This is one of the most captivating, intimate, no-holds-barred books of working-class history I have ever read. And it's a songbook, too!"
—David Rovics